Volcanoes

Written by Cheryl Palin
Illustrated by La Factoría Iluminada
with additional illustrations by Red Giraffe

Did you know that ...

... there are about 500 active volcanoes on land?

They are called *active* volcanoes, because they erupted in the past and they can erupt again. Some active volcanoes are always erupting.

Kilauea is an active volcano in Hawaii.

Kilauea is more active than any other volcano in the world. The island of Hawaii is growing bigger and bigger because of the eruptions.

Arenal is an active volcano in Costa Rica. It started erupting in 1939. It is still erupting. Tourists come to see the volcano at night.

There are also *dormant* volcanoes. These volcanoes are sleeping. They are dangerous too. They can wake up and erupt again.

Mount Fuji in Japan is dormant at the moment. The last time it erupted was in 1707.

Some volcanoes are *extinct*. Extinct volcanoes are volcanoes we think can't erupt again. But sometimes they wake up!

Anatahan is an island in the Pacific Ocean. Scientists believed the volcano on the island was extinct but on 11th May 2003 it erupted. The smoke was 12,200 metres high!

Vesuvius is an extinct volcano in Italy. It is a very famous volcano because there was a terrible eruption in 79 A.D. We know about the eruption from very old letters.

When Vesuvius erupted there was a lot of ash. The ash covered all the city of Pompeii. Only the roofs of the houses were not covered. Pompeii was a lost city.

In 1595, people discovered the city of Pompeii again. There were more excavations from 1863 to 1875. We can learn a lot about life in 79 A.D. from these excavations.

Vesuvius erupted about 36 times after 79 A.D. The last time it erupted was in 1944. Today, about one million people live and work in this area.

Did you know that ...

... there are lots more volcanoes under the sea?

Only one third of the world's active volcanoes are on land. The others are under the sea. The underwater volcanoes can grow so big that islands form.

An underwater volcano

The Galapagos Islands are volcanic islands. They are near the coast of Ecuador. There are 13 big islands, 6 smaller islands and lots of tiny islands and rocks. There are still eruptions in The Galapagos Islands. Fernandina and Isabela are the most active islands.

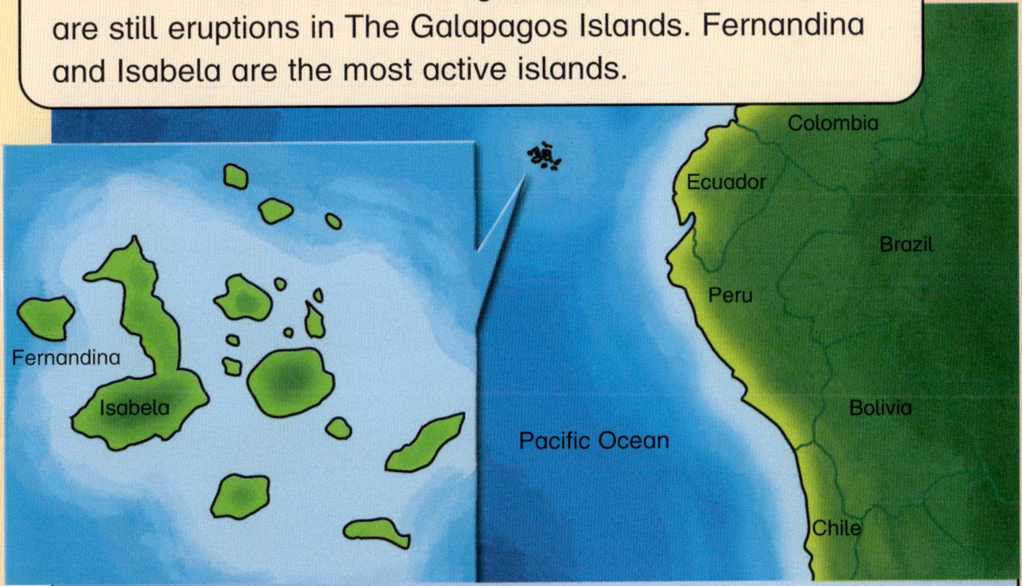

The Galapagos Islands

Did you know that ...

... Mauna Loa is bigger than any other volcano in the world?

Mauna Loa covers half of the island of Hawaii. Its Hawaiian name means 'Long Island' and it is a very long island! It is 120 kilometres long.

Mauna Loa measures 4 kilometres above sea level and it is another 5 kilometres to the sea floor. From its base under the sea, Mauna Loa is taller than Mount Everest.

Did you know that ...

... there are volcanoes in very cold places?

Antarctica has lots of volcanoes. Mount Erebus is an active volcano on Ross Island. It is bigger than the other active volcanoes in Antarctica. It is 3,794 metres high. Most of the volcano is under snow and ice.
There is also a volcano in Antarctica called

Mount Erebus

Did you know that ...

... you can have a mud bath in a volcano?

A mud volcano is formed by natural gas under the ground. The gas pushes the mud up and the mud dries in the sun. When more and more mud comes up, the volcano becomes taller and taller.

El Totumo is a mud volcano in the north of Colombia. It is only 15 metres high. People climb the volcano and lie in the mud. The mud has lots of minerals. People say it is very good for you.

After a mud bath you look very funny!

Did you know that ...

... Indonesia has more active volcanoes than any other country?

Indonesia has about 125 active volcanoes. Other countries with lots of active volcanoes are Japan and the USA.

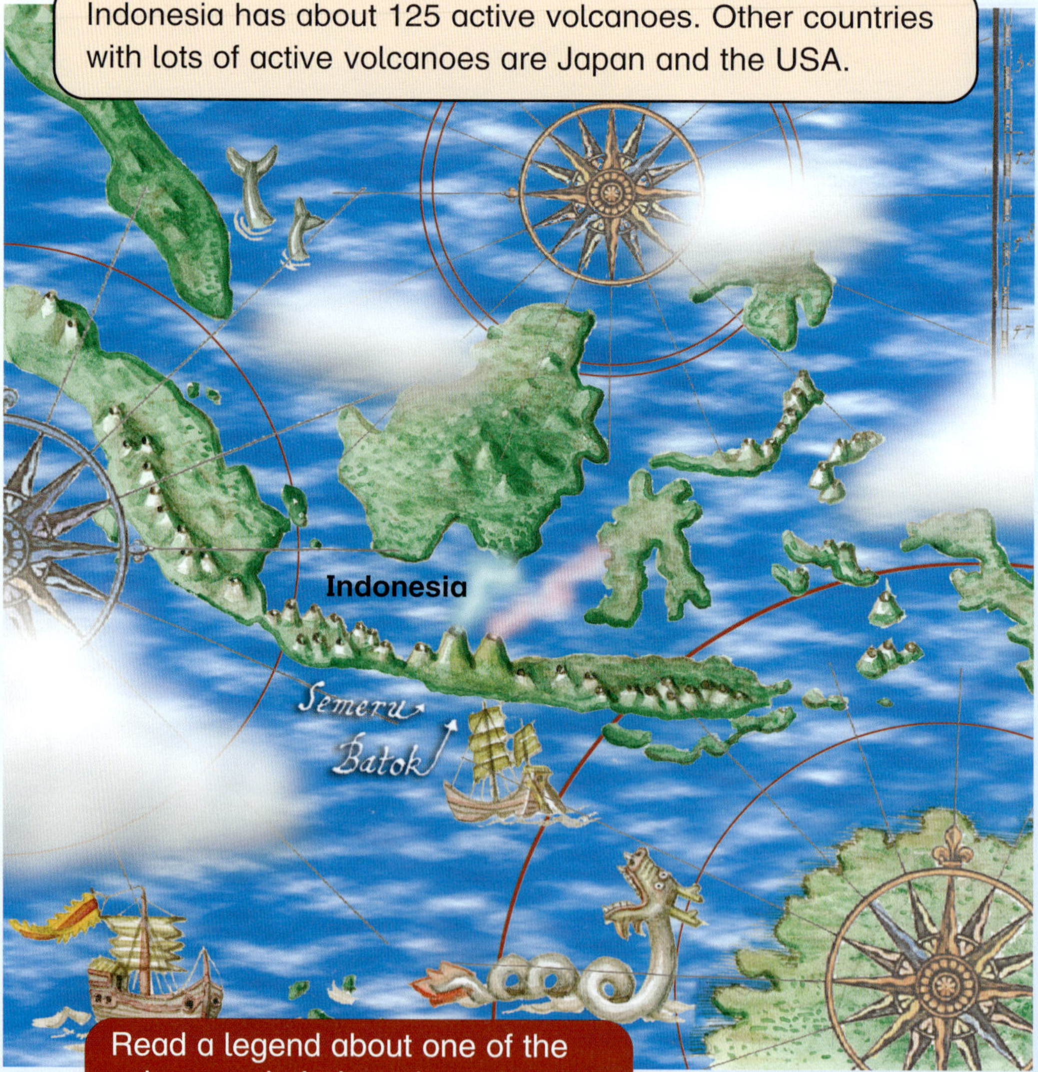

Read a legend about one of the volcanoes in Indonesia.

The legend of Batok Volcano

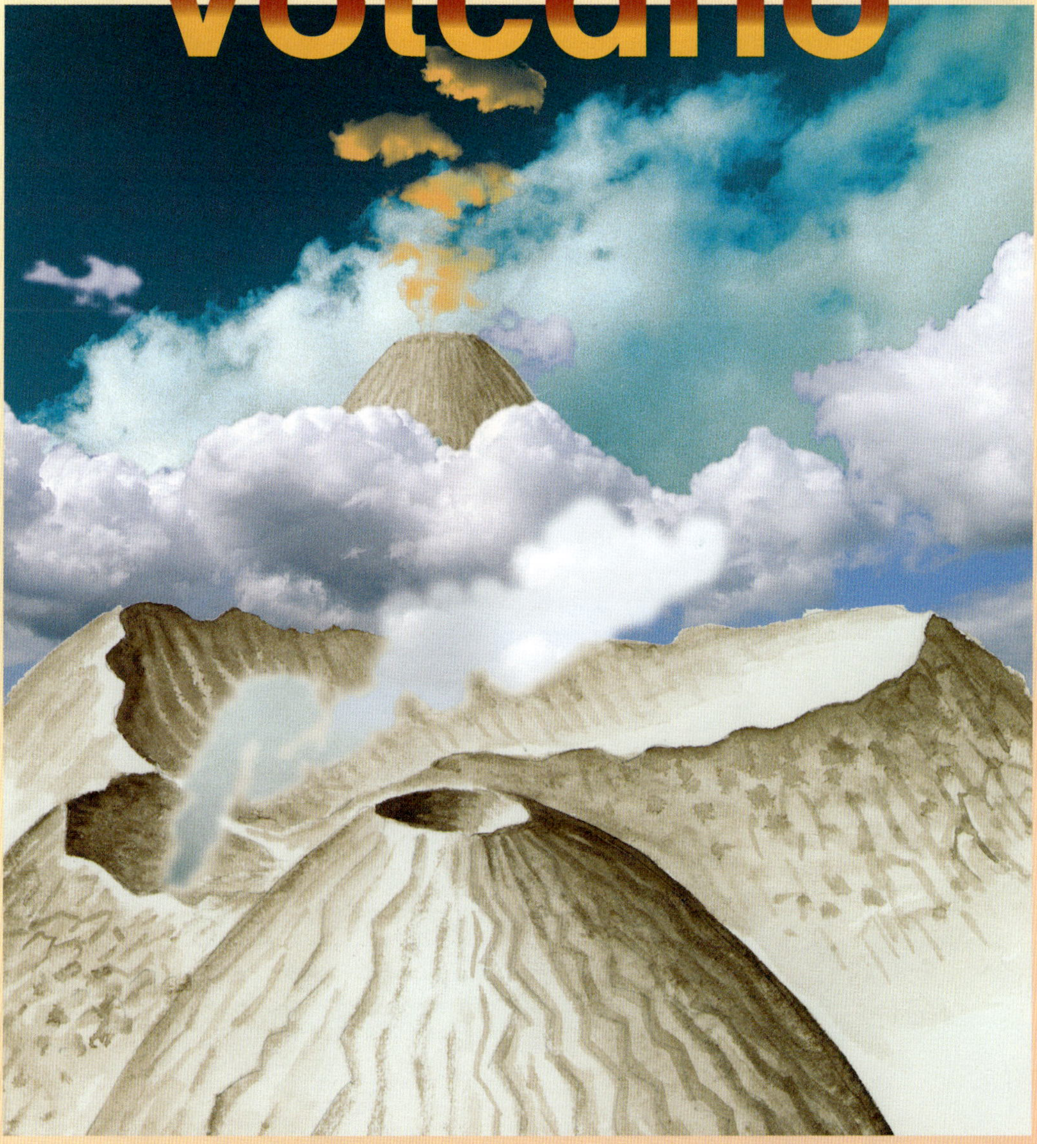

Written by Cheryl Palin
Illustrated by Francisco Meléndez

There are stories about volcanoes in many different countries. This is a legend about a volcano in Indonesia.

Once there was an ogre who lived in the countryside near Semeru volcano. The ogre lived alone and he was very happy. But one day the royal family travelled near his cave. Princess Siti wanted to see Semeru volcano. The princess looked at the volcano and the ogre looked at the princess.

From that day, the ogre loved Princess Siti.
He wasn't hungry ...

... and he wasn't tired.

He dreamed about the princess all day and all night.

Finally, the ogre walked to the royal palace. He asked the king for permission to marry his daughter. But the king laughed.

The ogre was very angry. He stayed in the palace doorway all day.

The ogre was a problem for the royal family. The king talked to the queen. Then he had a clever idea.

The ogre listened to the king's plan.
I want you to dig a hole ten metres wide. I want you to use this coconut shell. You've got one night to dig the hole. I want the hole finished by 6 o'clock in the morning.
Oh! That's very difficult! The coconut shell is very small.
You can start tonight at 7 o'clock.

The ogre loved the princess, so at 7 o'clock in the evening he started to dig the hole.

But the ogre worked very hard. He didn't stop. He wanted to marry Princess Siti.

At 4 o'clock in the morning, the hole was nearly finished. The king was very worried.
Oh no! The ogre is going to finish the hole in one night! I don't want the ogre to marry the princess! What can I do?
Then the king had another clever idea.
Come on! Quickly! It's time to get up and start your work! It's morning!
It's not time to get up! It's 4 o'clock.

But the servants did what the king said. They cleaned the palace and cooked the rice. The cockerels noticed the lights and the noise. They believed it was 6 o'clock. They started to crow.

The king tricked the ogre. The ogre believed it was 6 o'clock too. He was very tired and very disappointed. He stopped digging and he never finished the hole.

Now people say the crater is the ogre's hole and Batok Volcano is his coconut shell.
Yes. Look! That's Batok Volcano!
It's a great story!

Activities

1 Match the volcanoes with their locations.

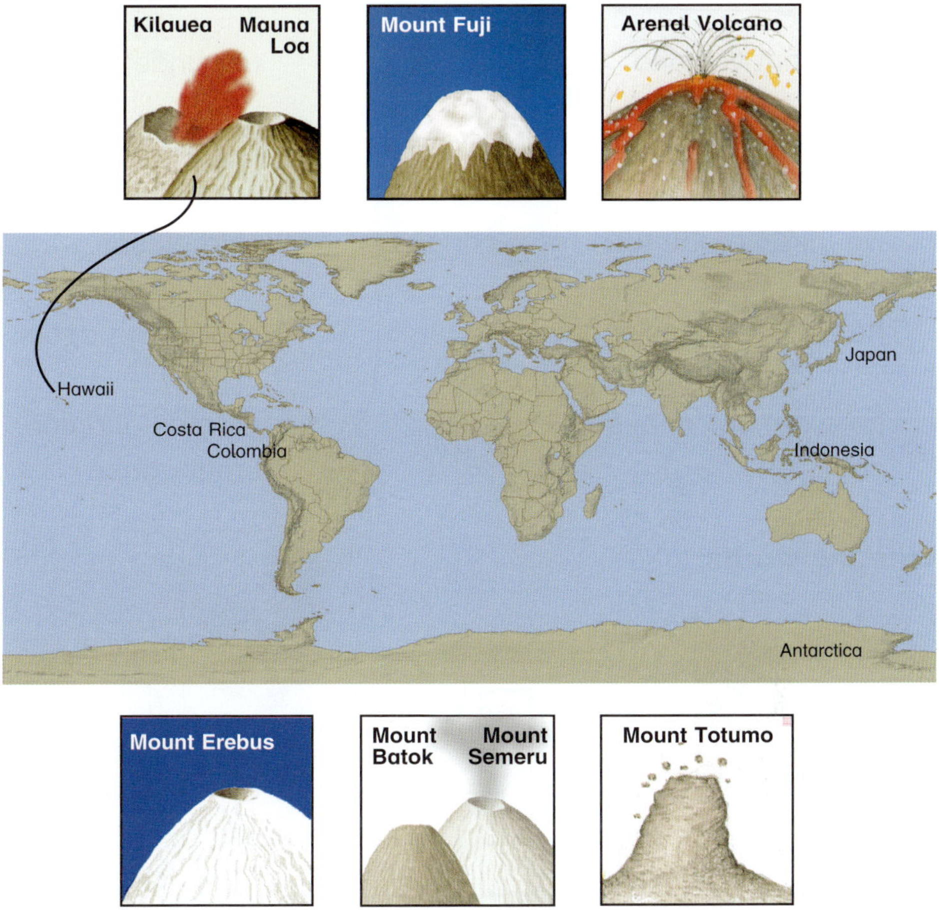

2 Look at the map in Activity 1 and write sentences.

1 Mauna Loa and Kilauea are in Hawaii.

2 Mount Fuji is __________

3 Arenal Volcano __________

4 __________

5 __________

6 __________

3 Match the beginnings and the ends of the sentences.

1 An active volcano	in Ecuador.
2 A dormant volcano	are under the sea.
3 An extinct volcano	is sleeping.
4 Two thirds of the world's volcanoes	cold places.
5 The Galapagos Islands are	can't erupt again.
6 There are volcanoes in	erupted and can erupt again.

4 Write the words.

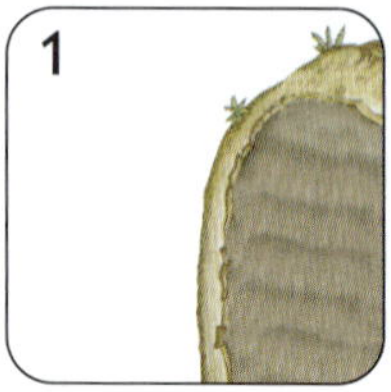

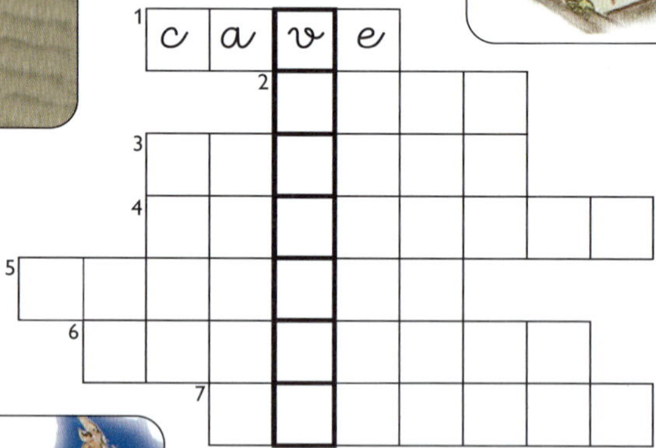

The secret word is ________________.

5 Number the pictures in order of the story. Write sentences.

started cooked worked ~~travelled~~
stopped laughed started was

The royal family travelled near the ogre's cave.

1

The ogre __________ very hard.

The king ______________________________.

The servants cleaned and _______________.

The cockerels ___________________ to crow.

The king ____________ very worried.

The ogre ________________ digging.

The ogre ______________ to dig.

6 Answer the questions.

1 Did the ogre love the princess? Yes, he did.
2 Did the king laugh at the ogre? ______________
3 Did the ogre use a coconut shell? ______________
4 Did the ogre finish the hole? ______________
5 Did the ogre marry the princess? ______________

7 Complete the summary of the story with the words in the box.

~~ogre~~	volcano	laughed	looked	hole
finished	travelled	stayed	asked	loved

Once there was an (1) ogre. The royal family (2) ______________ near his cave. Princess Siti looked at the (3) ______________. The ogre (4) ______________ at the princess. From that day the ogre (5) ______________ the princess. He (6) ______________ the king for permission to marry his daughter. The king (7) ______________. The ogre (8) ______________ in the palace doorway. The king asked the ogre to dig a (9) ______________ by 6 o'clock in the morning. The king tricked the ogre and the ogre never (10) ______________ the hole.

Bilingual Dictionary

Write the words in your language.

active	______	marry	______
bath	______	measure	______
beautiful	______	move	______
cave	______	mud	______
clever	______	nobody	______
cockerel	______	ogre	______
coconut	______	palace	______
countryside	______	princess	______
crater	______	push	______
dangerous	______	queen	______
daughter	______	rice	______
dig	______	rock	______
disappointed	______	royal	______
doorway	______	scientists	______
erupt	______	servant	______
eruption	______	smoke	______
extinct	______	space	______
Hawaii	______	talk	______
hole	______	tall	______
impossible	______	the USA	______
Indonesia	______	tourists	______
island	______	ugly	______
Japan	______	underwater	______
king	______	view	______
land	______	volcanic	______
laugh	______	volcano	______
legend	______	wake up	______
long	______	wide	______
louder	______	worried	______

Macmillan Education
4 Crinan Street
London N1 9XW
A division of Springer Nature Limited
Companies and representatives throughout the world

ISBN 978-1-3800-3783-1
ISBN 978-1-3800-3782-4 (International Edition)

First published 2005
This edition published 2019

Illustrated by Francisco Meléndez and Antonio Bretón at Factoría Iluminada, Zaragoza with additional illustrations by Red Giraffe.

The authors and publishers would like to thank the following for permission to reproduce their photographs:

Cover photo by Corbis ©Kevin Schafer

Alamy pp2 ©2001 Douglas Peebles Photography, 4 ©Hideo Korihara, 7 ©Culliganphoto, 9 ©Gary Cook; Alamy Stock Photo/World History Archive p8, Alamy Stock Photo/Idealink Photography p13; Corbis pp3 ©Kevin Schafer; Getty Images/iStock/Wildnerdpix p10, Getty Images/National Geographic/Jason Edwards p11; PhotoDisc/Getty Images/Cartesia p27.

Printed and bound in Great Britain by Bell and Bain Ltd, Glasgow

2023 2022 2021 2020 2019
10 9 8 7 6 5 4 3 2 1 Spain
10 9 8 7 6 5 4 3 2 1 International